Murmuration

~

Rod Picott

MEZCALITA PRESS, LLC
Norman, Oklahoma

FIRST EDITION
Copyright © 2018 by Rod Picott
All Rights Reserved

ISBN-13: 978-0-9994784-3-1

Library of Congress Control Number: 2018960467

No part of this book may be performed, recorded, thieved, or otherwise transmitted without the written consent of the author and the permission of the publisher. However, portions of it may be cited for book reviews—favorable or otherwise—without obtaining consent.

Cover Design: Stacie Huckeba
Cover Photo: Tasha Thomas

Visit Rod's website – www.rodpicott.com

MEZCALITA PRESS, LLC
Norman, Oklahoma

Murmuration

Rod Picott

Table of Contents

Acknowledgements vii

Alchemy 3
Atheist 4
In A Name 5
Day Drinking 6
Halloween 7
Lawn Tractor 8
Diamond 9
When The Darkness Comes 10
Swan Song 11
Fighting 12
The Waiting Room 13
Salute 14
Scars Everywhere 15
Thin 16
Lesser Gods 17
A Soldier's Boots 18
Leftovers 19
Murmuration 20
Subtraction 21
Making Love 22
Nature 23
Work 24
Extraordinary People 25
Desert 26
My Broken Back 27
The Last Chapter 28
Cigarette 29
Bought The Farm 30
Nature's Best 31
Yahtzee 32
Stranded 34

The Fox 35
Chicken Pot Pie 37
Replacement Parts 39
Nest 40
Fishing 42
The Gorge 43
Smoking 44
Still Winter In New England 45
Orbit Of Friends 46
Death In The Valley 47
Monk 48
Lucky Dog 49
The Cut 50
Wings 51
Cellar 52
Pets I've Known 53
Rock And Roll 54
Dreams End 56
Wedding 57
Checkbook 58
Tools 59
Paperboy 60
Caravaggio 61
The List Maker 62
Birds 63
Enemy 64
Begging 65
Drugs 66
Dreams 67
Impossible Angles 68
Fear 69
Dragonflies 71

Possible Outcomes 73
Critics 74
Worries 75
Slip Sliding Away 76
Closing Time 77
Buried 78
Mill 79
A Bath 80
List 81
Sleep Part 2 82
The Day After Thanksgiving 83
Rope 84
Wound 85
Yawn 86
Psychologist 87
Snakes In The Woodpile 88
Smarter People 89
Clock 90
Fleeing 91
Bad Conversation 92
The Green Bike 93
Waiting For The Coffee 94
Mowing 95
Worn 97
Conclusion 98

Author Bio 101

ACKNOWLEDGEMENTS

Thank you to:

Nathan Brown
Ashley Brown
Tasha Thomas
Jennifer Tortorici
Jamey Wood
Stephen Pulsford
Ron Rash
Nicholson Baker
Lloyd Picott
Lois Picott
Stacie Huckeba
Patty Griffin
Amanda Shires
Jim Harrison
Brian Koppelman for the six second writing class

Also by Rod Picott

Poetry
God in His Slippers

Short Stories
Out Past the Wires

Murmuration

Rod Picott

Alchemy

I have not invented a thing.
I only stir the paints
words
and stories
I've heard
back into the kettle.

Then I serve it up as my own gold.

Atheist

I'm an atheist
until the shooting starts
then of course
it all changes.

I was a scientist
until her hand touched mine
then I
was reborn.

I'm a cynic in black boots
until the end of the page
then I
wipe away the tear.

I don't believe in anything
I've ever believed in.
I'm an atheist
until the shooting starts.

In A Name

Picott is spelled Picot in French.
It means itchy scratchy,
as though you have a pox.
And I'm quite sure
for a few of my exes
this is a perfectly appropriate translation.

Day Drinking

It started with a beer
just to knock off a jagged corner
that kept snagging my mind.

There was the ghost of failure
shoving its shiv into my soft belly.

Then a whiskey short and neat
not so filling to knock the
sharpened metal from the ghost's hand.

Another beer to help with a short nap
and one more whiskey. Morpheus visited.

Weeks passed and so did
the beer and the whiskey.
Wine at night with television
until there was no accounting department.
They had all been dismissed.
The ledgers blank.

I don't want to know
how much I'm drinking.
I might prefer
the ghost with his knife.

Outside, the rain falls as soft
as the pillow beneath my head.
Inside, the whiskey
pours soft as the rain.

Halloween

My brother and I
with candy loot
walking the steep
length of Pearl St.

Fireball costume
Tweety Bird mask
Poor kids take
the disguise they're given

A rush of sneakers
A shove from behind
Two older kids
stole our collected treasures

And they are still out there
faces dark in tree shadows
A bright October moon
trying in vain to reveal them

Our mother's friend
from the rental across the street
gave us a few Reese's cups
to soften the loss.

I've hated Halloween ever since.

Lawn Tractor

I never change the oil.
I never clean the mower deck.
I don't even keep it out of the rain.

But I do thank this loud machine
for its single ability
to make it impossible for a short time to
answer my phone or speak with anyone.

There are long straight lines
of green to make
and now is the time I must make them.

Bless this 12-horsepower beast.

Diamond

The diamond in the ring
that he placed upon her hand
is simply the carbon
from ancient remains
the bones and branches
the death of ancestors
forgotten to time.
We all stand in line
to be crushed into
pretty little diamonds.

When The Darkness Comes

People gather up
what they are busied with
and turn to the
house and warmth.

There are faint outlines
of what approaches in the black night.
They don't want
to gamble a guess as it becomes late.

But some things are softer
in the not knowing.
So when the darkness comes
I stand awhile at the door –
Maybe it is love returning to me.

And not the wolves
the drunk neighbor
the thief or the beggar.
Maybe it's her
in her sundress stitched of hope.

Swan Song

She's waiting for her song now.
Through the thick dark pines it is barely audible.
The dog lies at her feet
and pricks his ears
when the wind is just right
and a sliver of a note comes through the door.

She's waiting to hear the tune of her now –
the melody that will be her exit.
Could it be on trumpet? Violin?
Or even the throaty soft scrape
of Louis Armstrong – who she loves dearly?
Will it be the coyote wail?
That would please her,
to think she has an animal spirit choir.

Her hands are branches,
her hair weeds
and she's getting closer.
She sits still,
looks out the dirty window panes
with her ears waiting.

She is in no hurry
but she is listening now
and waiting to hear her song.
She's ready to be sung away now
to her forever home.

Fighting

They made a ring
from clothesline
and sticks pounded into the soft ground.

Drunk uncles
tied boxing gloves
like whole turkeys onto the boys' hands.

"Ding ding" someone said.
And arms thin as sticks
threw punches until someone cried.

Then the aunts were angry
and the real fight began.
This fight had no punching
but also produced a loser.

The Waiting Room

Sitting in the waiting room I wonder:
How many here are dying and don't yet know?
Will someone be told today their time is ending?
Will the old man get an erection again?
Whose blood is poisoned and betraying them?
Why is the young black teen in handcuffs?
Which one of us has a tiny tell-tale ticking
or low rumble somewhere inside
that will expose a building void in their aliveness?
Who has bones long ago broken and fused?
Who will be cut open and rearranged inside?
Will someone leave with less of themselves –
a finger or a spleen?
Is there a heart thumping weakly
or with the unsteady beat of a junior high school
marching band snare drum?
There is trouble running through veins.
There is a weak vessel about to give way
to slurred speech and inability to point at the
doughnut he wants.
He will mumble "Maple Round" but will in fact say
"Mbbb Owwww."
There is much trouble here and worry and fear.

And yet someone is finding out
that the sperm has indeed reached the egg.
This is the happiest day of their lives
even though it contains
an unnamable and distant fear.

Salute

It's nice to stand here
in the rain
with the heavy drops
pattering the deck

We've become
too comfortable
far removed
from nature

With our ponchos
and hats
our raincoats
our catalogs

So right now
I'll stand here
wet as a foal
and howl

under my breath
a salute
to the ancient
blood in my veins

Scars Everywhere

His fingernails were black with dirt.
His hair a greasy crown,
fists a permanent curl
of chewed knuckles.

He told lies through thick lips
but darting wary eyes
told the truth –
that you don't know
when the next punch comes.

I'm guessing they were Catholic
with all those siblings
wearing the shame of that family name.
A dark-eyed sullen mother
always belly-full with another.
She walked disturbingly slow
down the sidewalks
as if inviting derision
for her eternal natal display.

The father – a grim faced silent steel
10 penny nail of anger.
Seldom seen but leaving his imprint
on the faces of his children,
and on the stretched belly
of his seemingly impenetrable wife.
Scars everywhere.

Thin

He hides behind himself,
or thinks he does.
But he's too thin
to see
that he's not hidden much.

So we all see
the skyscraper of lies
looming above and behind –
blocking out the sun.

He's drinking
again.

Lesser Gods

Golden red light in the morning.
Impossible blue at its falling.
We measure our turns by the arc
that quickens with age.

How many times around the wheel
before the clicking stops?

The green busies the spring.
The wasps busy the summer.
The leaves busy the autumn.
And the tire chains bite into the winter.

We forgot all our prayers
to the yellow orb.
Centuries ago it must
have had ringing ears
and well-appointed garments,
a crown perhaps.

But now she's been reduced
to a simple clock
counting our days
as we pray to lesser gods
on pixel screens.

A Soldier's Boots

He was deeply tanned.
His boot was resting on the howitzer.
The boys around him were smiling.
"We couldn't wait to go kill."
Is what he told me once.

But years can reshape you slowly
into a different animal.
And he says now
"They brainwash you –
make you something you're not."

So like an un-sprung trap
your future is waiting
to sink its teeth into
whatever leg trips the metal.

There are fewer things worth
turning boys into death merchants
than we think is what he thinks now.

We take the least valuable
and turn them into something of value –
things to fill the hole up.
So that we can walk easily
over their backs
to the well to fill our buckets
with cool clean water.
This is what he knows now
that his boot has been off the gun for awhile.

Leftovers

We had the great feast
then the riches turned
to scraps.

This is the trouble
with too much
when you don't have enough
to have too much.

When you have enough
to have too much
there are no scraps.

There is only
the clean polished
cherry federalist table
with its fine spindle legs
empty and ready again
to receive the finery and silver.

But in this house
there was a skyscraper of Tupperware
filled with scraps
and ready for brown bags.

Murmuration

When the dark kite of birds soars
its shape shifting blanket
folding and unfolding in the sky
my heart lifts to join it in a small way.

The impossible beauty
of simple cooperation without thought
is more thrilling
than fireworks.

The sun lies down in the distance
throwing golden coins of light.
The ancient trees reach to him
with their praying hands
and the starlings perform
their mysterious dance

for an ever dwindling audience
that prefers the crash of metal
and the shattering of glass –
I suppose because the audience are our children.
The sun, the trees, the birds are our elders.
And we don't call our parents much.

Subtraction

The years crawled across her face
slower than a day allows you to see.
Time leaves razor thin winking valleys
that widen without notice.

Unlike the great burst of the beautiful oak in spring
it is the slow diminution of leafy green
that begins when the summer seems still strong
and hard.

Strong and hard no longer apply.
She moves very slowly now.
Nicotine yellow fingers
can no longer handle the heft of a quilt
and are deposed to hand towels and placemats –
simple single squares of cloth cut crookedly
from larger squares of cloth.

To make a smaller thing
from a larger thing
has replaced
making a larger thing
from smaller things.

Everything now is subtraction.

Making Love

Hammer the metal
until it's shining and hard.
Then beat it
into the shape of a bowl
that can hold
all that you will need
to combine.

And if you get the mixture just right –
you each put in the right
powders and oils,
you can live on it for
the rest of your journey.

But most people
put in too much of one thing
too little of another.
There is no recipe that survives.
Nothing is written down
to pass along.
You just guess at it.

Nature

We cut and hack
at her limbs,

tie her hair back,
starve her into shapes

that suit our
simple minds.

But she doesn't
want any of it.

And tries to tell us
with every weed and razor thorn.

She is an unruly child
and will have her way
in the end.

Work

I don't really care
that much for food.
It doesn't make much difference
what I eat.

What I want is to be able to work.
I want huge slices of time that are my own.
I want to gorge myself with writing and reading.
I want to drink all the language and chew endlessly
on the words stuck on my mouth
to spit out the words that don't work
until I find one as delicious and tender as I desire.

Sometimes I want bitter words
or sour descriptions that make heads turn away.
Sometimes I want sweet succulent words
that make my mouth water.

So I don't really care
that much for food.
You can see
it doesn't make much difference
what I eat.

Extraordinary People

There are special people out there.

Bob Dylan wrote "Blowing in the Wind."
A song so preternatural it seems
to always have existed.
One day he simply wrote it.

John Glenn strapped himself to a rocket
and flew to outer space
before anyone knew that your head wouldn't ignite
when you arrived there.

Marlon Brando reinvented
the art of acting like a matchstick
reinventing a dry forest.
He stopped pretending.

Jackie Robinson shoveled his rage
into his bones, muscles and the sting of his bat.
He was a man with grace and dignity.
He force-fed the truth
to a country starving on ignorance
and burned himself down in sacrifice.

There is also my father who taught himself to read
so that he could get a better job to raise his family.
He worked every shift he was ever offered,
helped every cousin move
because he owned a pick-up truck.
This is also extraordinary.

Desert

I throttled the hot engine
until the desert floor turned to dust.
Cacti were ghosts on the horizon
specters leaning down from ancient burial grounds
but I was untouched by their boney fingers.
The sun had long since dropped below the hills
and the cool of night was beginning its slow descent
like a blanket warm from the dryer.
Long ago these lands teemed
with deer, bobcats and coyotes
but here now
just this oiled machine spitting and coughing
down the long ribbon of black-grey highway
gave indication of movement.

My Broken Back

The ladder slid down the house.
I could hear the aluminum against the brick
as I rode it down – shshshshsh.

I thought:
I hope I don't spill all this expensive paint.
I spilled all the expensive paint.

When the ride was over I was curled, writhing in pain.
My legs were trapped in the ladder's teeth.

I couldn't move. The pain was gutting.
I thought I might throw up.
I couldn't breathe fully.

I crawled to the car. But it was a slow crawl.
Not like when you give a child a donkey ride.

I drove the 20 miles home because
I had no insurance.
Then I crawled from the car inside to my bed.

It took weeks until I could stand up.
The pain was shocking and impenetrable.

Years later I had insurance.
When the chiropractor looked at the x-ray
He said "Oh..."

The Last Chapter

When the sun
drops its heavy bag
of gold coins
behind the curtain of pines
and two crows bicker
from the telephone pole
the chicken pie
arrives fuming mad
from the oven
and we all sip wine
from coffee mugs
and pretend that
everything is fine.

The bottles of pills,
lotions, potions, poisons,
ointments, salves and
wet nubs of cigarette amputations
tell a different story.

This book is in its final
chapter and soon
the last curled and withered
words will burn up quickly –
dry leaves aflame in the late autumn cold.
I hope she'll be wearing
a warm coat when the last of the night air
comes stealing in.

Cigarette

That skinny stick between the yellowed fingers
of my grandmother as she drove
her Chevy Impala – the green one.
The cigarette made it nearly impossible
for her to gather coins for the toll.

My mother loved you even more.
I once asked, "What if you end up
in an oxygen tent gasping for air?
Will it have been worth it?"
(No pause)
"Oh yes. I love to smoke."

Bogart looked good with one.
Bacall too, as her thin frame
leaned in the doorway.
Keith Richards isn't Keef without one.
Bukowski liked those bidis
from India that he kept re-lighting.

The only thing I can say for myself
is that they allow you some time to think,
a natural pause,
a few minutes that are filled
as you wait to do the thing you came to do.

But Bacall really did look good
striking a match
with one between her lips.
Don't try to say she didn't.

Bought The Farm

She resented him
for buying the farm
that took her away
from her people.

She resented the cows
the long season of haying
the fecund smell
that never left the place.

She was angry
that he bought the cows
that he bought the farm
until he bought the farm.

Nature's Best

The snow falls
light as dust
big airy flakes
spilling from
the heavens.

The oceans groan
and spit
our collected
history
onto the sand.

Our beginning
an explosion
of particles
and dust
blasted infinitely
outward.

Her kiss
soft as
a fallen petal
from a lily
left too long
unattended.

Yahtzee

We play Yahtzee.
The game requires no skill
no memory
or strategy of note.

She cackles and shrieks
when she rolls a Yahtzee.
His is a game of quiet obfuscation.
Mine a game of attrition
with the clock I can see on the stove.

Outside the conifers lay bets.
The crystalline sky is cold
and is spilled with diamonds.
The nocturnal beasts prowl.

Sixes look good.
Fours are rare.
You must get the top filled in
is his creed.
Those 35 points will win
you the game –

unless she shrieks
and throws her hands up.
In that case you are doomed
and might as well
scoop some generic vanilla ice cream
and go all in – shooting for those five matching dice.

An old story is retold.
A new complaint is unfurled.
Insincere comical accusations hurled.

I call him Charles Nelson Reilly
in his ridiculous oversized reading glasses
and call her The Muppet in her fuzzy blue overcoat.
They love this teasing attention.
This is the way we have always been
and it must remind them of our history.

The bad, the angry, exploded then hidden away.
The good, the love in teasing phrases with just the
faintest scent of the hidden away
on the greasy axle of laughter as we play Yahtzee.

Stranded

When I was a child
there was no escaping
my own strange interior map.

The directions held me captive
in fear, sadness
and dark frightening hedgerows.

The school sent me to the psychiatrist
because they thought,
"Well something is wrong with this one."

And of course there was
something wrong
but not the thing
that they thought was wrong.

It was simply
that I was not the same as the rest,
though none of us are
but I was coloring too far
outside the lines.

And that is not allowed.

The Fox

Two crows split the sky
into thirds of blue.
An infinitely small satellite
of white dust
danced in slow motion
above the green
and uncut grass.

Cigarette smoke
and bitter dark coffee
say it's morning here.
A list of the day's work
ticks off in my ears
a metronome.

Later on
while I push the lawnmower
and it chews the lawn
into cud
from under the barn
the fox long unseen
limps into view.

I stare at her.
She stares at me.
Her limp is worse now
in the three years since
I saw her last.

She has grown old and slow
hobbles on three legs
stares at me.
I stare at her.

Then I push again
and my back stiffens
and my hip freezes
and I find it hurts to walk.
She stares at me and I stare at her.

She says to me, "I can't run.
Don't ask me to run."
And I say, "No, you don't have to run.
I'm just pushing this red machine around
in your yard for awhile."

And so she hops to the tree line
then disappears into the low leaves to wait
while I mow her yard.
And I think to myself
"I'll cut it low.
Then she can find the voles easier to catch."
And I start pushing
and I'm very slow.
I'm an old mottled fox.

Chicken Pot Pie

He sits. Sometimes sleeps.
In a lawn chair behind the farmhouse.

The long days have shortened to minutes.
The birds have collected on the power lines.

He counts.
Five crows. Twelve chickadees.
One woodcock and a pheasant.
His eyes deeply lined
creased by years with a welding torch
are still sharp.

The porcupine never stood a chance.
But it never should have chewed on his shed.
The squirrel never had a chance.
It was stealing from the chickadees.

The gloves of leaves on the maple tree are red.
The coins of leaves on the poplar are gold.
A bit of rust is making an advance
up the aluminum leg of the lawn chair.
He counts again but falls asleep before reaching
twelve. One bird flies away.

We wrestled the plywood onto the roof.
I cursed with the sharpness of a ka-bar blade.
The senile rafters joke of math eluding my screws.
Splinters laughed into my hands.
The old man handed wood trim and drip edge up.

Impossibly slow.
I sucked my breath in to carry the extra minutes
every timorous movement the old man took.
Every crooked cut was delivered on the wobbly legs
of young gone brittle with years.

In the steaming black fly air – hammers pounded,
saws chewed into sticky cheap pine, tar paper rolled,
blades ripped and the shed grew a new roof.

The only conversation was in
numbers and sharp curses
until squared and true
the new asphalt shingles heated in the summer
of the fading northeastern-western sky.

Two beers each
from forty feet away
staring at the work.

"Christ it looks good."
"I hope that one shingle lays down."
"It's gonna last longah than I will."
"I suppose it will."
"Your muthah made chicken pot pie."
"It does look pretty square."
"I ain't trying to build the Taj Mahal. Your muthah made chicken pot pie."

Replacement Parts

The belt that spun the blades
was cracked.
The starter refused to
make a spark.

These are things replaced
without complaint
just bolts to loose
joints to ache.

But her beside me
in the night
the touch of hands
soft and white.

There is no path
to gather back
the thing
forever lost.

No catalog
to order back
this thing
forever lost.

Nest

Her room is very small.
It was painted white but has soured nicotine yellow.
A Folgers coffee can holds
the graveyard of cigarettes.
We joked conspiringly about the yellowing because
I was the painter.
I wanted her to know this is fine with me –
the nicotine yellow.

There is the all-seeing small fan perched on the sill –
a breathy bird blowing smoke through the window
screen. Summer and winter.

Her fingers busy with needle, thread
and patches of cloth.
The sewing machine's oiled hum
convinces the wide pine floor to hum along.
The room hums too. Her one song.

She is bent where she was straight.
Her head bobbles on a neck weak from some
malady. An old and loose spring somewhere inside
holds her together – and the sewing.

Her hand's relentless stitching
knuckles hard as bark somehow keeps her whole.
She is a quilt.
She is pieces from many years
held together by a thread so thin
other birds would ignore it for their nests.
But in her nest – this is all that's needed –
the invisible thread
and the sewing machine I bought her for Christmas.

It's an old machine. An anvil of weight
to hold her down lest she float away.
Her companion.
She likes the old things.
I like them as well.

Fishing

The hook
was set deep.

When I look
at my adult words

I see a child
deeply hurt embarrassed and alone

trying desperately
to remove the black barb sunk into his flesh

that he can carry on in the small boat he built

trying to catch the rest
of what might be good
left in his life.

The Gorge

He was once enormous
a steaming beast of a train before you
but he has left the station
has become a rumble from across the river
a faraway whistle.
There is distance in his voice now.

When we talk on the phone
there are pauses
as he waits for
the dimming synapses
to spark
for the wheels to turn to motion.

We all go in the same direction.
We are all dying in slow motion
as we barrel down
the dirty tracks of this world.

Somewhere out there
the rails stop over a thousand-foot gorge.
That is where
two hundred tons of locomotive
flies weightless.
A gnat into oblivion.
There is a distance in his voice now.

Smoking

She blows smoke
from a hand rolled menthol
into the yellow fan.

Day and night
the endless stream
of smoke blows.

The television brings news
from a world far away
from her now.

With each orange morning
she waits for the end –
she has been too tired for too long.

This is how it ends.
In the flickering blue
of a small television

with smoke blown into
a cheap Chinese fan
thick scars where
new hips were added

like retread tires
to get just a few
more miles from her.

Still Winter In New England

The beavers
silky wet
and not quite so busy now
have given us a place to skate
that is flat as a serving tray.

Aluminum lawn chairs
claim shoveled parking spots
and you do not touch
someone else's lawn chair.
Ever.

The radio announcer
is very angry about The Bruins playoff chances.
It's apparently the goalie's fault
or the defensive line.
It's everyone's fault.

Morning coffee never tasted so good.
The sky was never this gray.
Your skin was never this translucent.
I can see right through you.

But because you are from New England
I still don't know what you're thinking.
Except that you wish spring would arrive soon
and unpack his suitcase of green garments.

Orbit Of Friends

There are a few.
Pluto and Jupiter.
From time to time
there are small gatherings.
But you don't confess much anymore
and the confessions
have become less fun to spill out
and to hear.

All the planets
are moving slowly
away from the sun
in wider arcs.
There is less summer
and more winter now.

And you look back
at the other planets
that once seemed so close
and realize
you could never exist
in that other atmosphere.

So you float out there
mostly alone
with just a friendly wave
on occasion
as another planet passes by.

Death In The Valley

Mr. Hitchens had died.
He was not quite old.
There is a lot of potato salad
to be made by neighbors
and delivered to his shrewish wife
who is thrilled
by the attention.

His ungrateful children
are driving in
from out of state.
Such a bother to use
time off for ceremonies.

There was a strange woman
hovering at the edge
of the small crowd
at Mr. Hitchens' burial.

And there is a will to sort.
It will come as a surprise to most
that Mr. Hitchens has left it all
to a young woman
with whom he had a long loving affair
filled with laughter and joy
love-making without judgment or expectation.

She will remember his gentle touch
and their secrets for a very long time.

Monk

Today is the day
I promised myself
I will do all the things
I don't want to do.

I'll do all the math
and filling out forms.
I'll sit at the desk
and eat only small bits.

Today I'll be a monk
in my room.
But today
I'll do it on purpose
unlike all the other days.

The other days
my hand is forced by fate
and the lack of a lover to lie beside
and busy my troubled mind.

Lucky Dog

I was chained to a tree.
I watered and nurtured it
until it was too tall
and too strong to pull down.

Then I put the tiny teeth of a saw to it.
And now I am running
through the neighborhood
growling at everything
I once cowered from.

The Cut

I'm told she fell.
I asked if it was
because of the
drinking.

There was a pause
so I knew before
he answered the
question.

For all her worry
about her son's
own slow vodka
poisoning

she has taken
up the very
gun she fears
most.

And it has left
a deep ribbon
of red under her
eye.

She nearly
didn't miss this time.

Wings

Some are born with wings.
It's a glorious thing
to watch them
cut through the high thin air.

I had to make mine.
They said –
"You'll never fly with those wings.
That's just some canvas and leather
and grommets you've scrapped together."

But I had secretly tethered
my own thin bones
and muscles to the contraption.
And while I might not go very high –

I fly.

Cellar

The salt box house sat
at the top
of a small hill.

Against all rules of physics
the dirt cellar
flooded
every spring.

My father was in his boots
awake all night
bailing with
buckets.

No money
for a simple pump.
The sentinel
of the furnace.
His bucket a shield.

This was back when
men did these things –
stayed awake all night long
bailing with a bucket
then went to
work in the morning.

I suspect
he was bailing
to save more than the furnace.

Pets I've Known

The dog's nose was a wet
pink eraser.

The cat displayed
itself – an exhibitionist.

The other cat
was a bratty and cruel acrobat.

The other dog
was small, black and wiggly.

A turtle
had no personality
aside from his hygiene which
smelled of lacking.

A hamster
hung from his cage.
Tiny arms
stretched tight by his girth-y middle.

The St. Bernard
was the best.
Not smart, not overly pleasant,
but she was the
most recognizable
as *one of us*.

Rock and Roll

In spite of all the thieves
the deviants and businessmen
in suits with switch blades
in their pockets;
in the end
it was also Rock and Roll
that helped free people.

The music re-wired
our grid and made possible
a screaming homosexual
black pompadour singing
about fucking
on the Philco.
Your sister
loved it and played
the song over and over.

Then the white people
tried the same chords
and made millions.
So Chuck Berry said
"Cash money brown bag
your hand to mine."
Sitting like Ceasar
in his Cadillac.

Before the bankers and businessmen
poured water on the fire
we all danced
glorious and wild eyed
around the burning coals
hot and dangerous.
We stepped right up to the edge
with sweat pouring down our faces.

Little Suzie with her hand in her panties
played the record over and over.

No wonder her parents were scared.

Dreams End

The tennis racket
was a Les Paul
electric guitar
in his hands
when The Who
played a concert
in his bedroom
and he was Pete Townshend
ripping into chords
with bloodied hands
and cutting Rock and Roll
into a mystical new cast
until his mother
yelled up the staircase
that the Salisbury steak
was ready and his father
needed help with the shoveling.

Wedding

She in her lovely dress
he in his handsome suit
are agreeing
to get into a car
with no brakes
at the top of a mountain.

Checkbook

Mom:
You could tell when there was trouble
by the sound of the dishes
blasting like firecrackers.
Pans were small cannons
and they were put down
where she wanted them and they didn't *dare* move.
A glass would crack and bubbles
of dish soap would turn pink with blood
in the dirty water.
This seemed to bring some calm.
It's unsatisfying to have something break
and have no blood to show for it.
She always made sure there was something
to show for it.
You could tell when there was trouble
by the sound of the dishes.

Dad:
With the checkbook open
doing the math
things always add up to *something*
even when they don't add up.
Tip-toe past the table and down the hall
hold your breath count to twenty.
Don't forget
to be very, very quiet.
There are things in the balance now
and the belt is very near
and these things always add up to *something*.

Tools

The hammer hits
the highest nail.
The spade bites into
the highest dirt.
The screwdriver twists its tongue
into the jaw of the intractable screw.
And I sit here sipping coffee
holding a Uniball pen
worrying that I will never
make a thing
that's beautiful enough.

Paperboy

It was colder than
I'd ever known.
The snow was piling
in huge white waves
motionless in their threat.

I handed a woman
the newspaper
then passed out
in her doorway.

She brought me inside
and my feet thawed,
the blood returned to
my head.

Then I went back out
into the storm
to bring everyone the news.
This small kindness is buried
in my memory yard.

Caravaggio

How is it that a hand
so steady and refined
a hand that could throw
shafts of light
like God himself
from simple paint
could also be the hand
on the knife
that pierced the flesh
and sent another man
to his bed of dirt?

Why does God give away
his gifts
like random presents
at an office Christmas party?

I'll ask if I get the chance.
There are some other things
I need to take up with him
as well –
missing keys,
a lost wallet,
my lousy sense of pitch.
Bombs falling on children.
Things like that.

The List Maker

They are all lined up
the little jobs of today
in a column.

Why is it so much more
pleasurable to pull
the black marker through them
and make a ladder
on the paper
rather than a different code?
I do not know.

I'm climbing down
the ladder of things
to get done.

At the end
I'm safely on the ground again
with a bottle of red wine.
My feet are sure enough
on the floor
that drinking
will not cause me to fall
down the ladder.
I've already reached the bottom.

Birds

A whisper of black wings
in the distance
pitches and spins.

A mystery of distance
direction
and circumstance.

Watching your earthbound inelegance
from a telephone pole
is a snickering crow.

Do they know the utter
unfettered-ness
of their miracle?

Enemy

He's here in the shadows.
Doubt works quietly.
He is a weed choking out
the wildflower that reaches
for the cool spring rain
and the warmth of the sun.

He says "It's not possible.
"You are a fool. You don't have
the hard muscle or the blind will."

But on better days
I cut him low to the dirt.
I silence his advance.
And give all the wild elements
of the world to the dandelion
that it can glow
in all its simple bright yellow.

Begging

Her insides were turning over on themselves
in a cruel wrestling match.
Still she begged for more vodka,
"Please…" in weak sobs.

The old man near her steels himself
refusing to dig the sharp
edge of his spade into
her dirt bed says "No."

An old woman's tears
at war with the gentleness
of an old man's anemic will.
In the end it was no match.

Though he held out for a while
she had gathered her soldiers
of pain and sorrow
at the front lines for many years
and overran the old man's
rusted artillery with ease.

A day later she drank deep
into the night from her attic room
no longer in tears and numb to the roiling in her gut.

Downstairs an old man's thumbs knitted the air.
A dog lay against him in the television's warm glow.
He slept in short dreams. His boots on, keys nearby.
His thumbs knitting without knowing.

Drugs

When you finally come down
(or back)
from all the drugs
there is the profound disappointment
that you are not the you
you thought you were for a few days.
And you are – in fact –
the same clod of dirt
you left behind before your flying act.

This is the trouble.
In your dreams you are brave and wise,
daring and shrewd.
But back here the brakes come on
and you are idling at the same red light
you left behind –
Dunkin Donuts on your left
Huffy Muffler on the right.

You are far away
from the high thin pines
that scatter the elevations
you were exploring
with your Bowie knife and canteen,
searching out the wonders of nature,
prepared for the wolverine
and embracing the animal inside,
the wild-eyed version of yourself.

Dreams

I dreamt so sharp that
I might as well have been awake.

The blade cut just as deep
as she told me over and over
that I was a joke to her.

Then I woke
and used her words like gasoline
to fire my work.

I hammered rusty nails,
flew the ink across the page,
I lifted huge stained beams into place
and tilled the black fecund ground.

She was there,
an enemy in my dream.
But here where the skin meets the spade?
I am king.
Dreams be damned.

Impossible Angles

The news is
that she was strangled.
She thought
they wanted her
to party with them.
And they did.

But there are people
whose idea
of a celebration
holds the idea
that they must
purge their rage.

And so she was found
by the railroad tracks.
A tiny woman
reduced to a body
of impossible angles.

She was not waiting
for the train.

Fear

Her resentment was
that he was not
the type she wanted.
She bought antiques
then adorned them
with flimsy appliqué she bought
from the department store.

He wanted no part
of museums
and scoffed at
intellectual pursuit
with the bitter anger
only the truly poverty-ravaged
and unschooled know.
A can of beer in one hand,
the other hand – a curled fist.

But an intoxicated meeting
of cells had connected them.
Then a wedding of sorts.
A weekend honeymoon
at Niagara Falls
where the water was as frozen
as her heart to him
and just as unyielding.

I do not think he knew
what he did not know.

That all he had to do
was to lose some of his past
to make room for a new future
that might include
some scraps of the things he feared –
antiques,
a few books,
a museum,
a conversation.

So terrifying – those things…

Dragonflies

She took me to her spot on the Brazos.
A dragonfly landed – delicate as a thread
on the bare finger of a stick
that was reaching up out of the dark water.

His wings were fringe on an ancient doily,
hand stitched by an elderly English housekeeper
named Edna or Dorothy.

I trained the dragonfly to land on my hand.
Then I walked him onto my nose
where he sat seeming contented
as long as I breathed slowly
a circus trick for nobody in the middle of wild Texas.

We played in the water.
We hooked and released a few small fish
while standing on a sand bar
casting into the shadowy good spots.

Her grandfather's land rolled out
all the way from the cattle-less pasture to the river.
The shape-shifting river kept its name, the Brazos,
in spite of its arms and legs taking new length, depth
and geometry with each rain.

This was her favorite spot.
It was not my favorite spot but
it was my favorite of her favorite spots.
I loved that she loved the place.

It didn't bother me to be one
of several boys and men she took there.
These things just are.
We had our time there
and that was *our* time.

The rest is for others to decipher.
It belongs in the map of someone else's memory.
But the dragonflies are mine to keep.
I'm keeping the dragonflies.

Possible Outcomes

The lawyer says that
there is a chance
that he might
do a year.

And

The lawyer says that
even though he
assaulted his wife,
he might get lenience.

I don't know
which
would be worse.

Critics

You don't have the tools
to even open the box I made
so I don't have any fear
of the butter knife you wave around.

You are resigned to searching
for your bottle of wasp spray
while we build our paper nests
filled with stingers.

It's true.
The last nest was bigger
and contained more wasps
and more danger.

But you still stand
twenty feet away
and spray from a distance
nervously seeking the best angle
with no one watching

then shout "Look!
I've killed the wasp!"
while we are already busy
building a new home
in the high crook
of an ancient church called art.

Worries

There is a single steel string
on an old guitar.
The rest of the strings
long since lost to rust.
Silent broken hairs.

The wolf cub left behind
its broken limb hanging
and the rest of him
jerking madly to keep up.

A quilt made from patches
of work shirts.
A square patch with her son's name
stained with oil
for sale at the Goodwill
$3.50.

Things are just things.
Without your grandfather's hands
your mother's worry
your distant lonely aunt's
too many hours
in front of the television.

Slip Sliding Away

She says "Yeah!"
in the middle of my sentence
when there is nothing yet
to respond to.

And her emotions
don't reflect
the subject at hand.

She only has two reactions:
Something is the greatest ever.
Something is the worst ever.

"I'm so proud!"
Or she cries softly
with intermittent wails.

She is starting to slip away.
And we all go in the same direction.
Of course we do.

But her last miles
are a long dirt road
the engine light on
with no gas station in sight.

On the skinny arm
reaching from a tree,
a crow waits patiently.

Closing Time

I close down my dreams.
Slowly – I lower the lid.
I'm older now.
Years have brittled my bones.
My worries are changing course
like a river unable
to contain itself
and spreading its long fingers
taking new ground.

My heart aches now
for what I didn't know then.
Time to fix things is running out.
The blade is dull,
the hammer misses the nail,
the wrench loses its grip and the elbow
smashes into the ground.
The bolt is stripped.

There is no healing.
There is only scarring.
There is no dealing.
Only being dealt.
There will be no accounting.
There will only be
a long erasing
of all I have ever written.

Buried

Deep inside
is the love
I once had to give.

In a salty cave
it was left behind
to be cured.

I dug it up later
but it no longer
tasted sweet.

A dead man's
dream unburied
to be found
dry and crumbling.

Mill

The mill has closed.

They handed out the slips of paper
that told them
they would no longer
be eating a flank steak on Friday night.

Everything grows small now.
The cupboard supplies,
the plate of food,
the drip of gasoline into the tank,
and the drawer of new school clothes.

Except the whiskey.
The whiskey flows in rivers now.

A Bath

His scent was everywhere.
Followed him like an old cur.
An old man now long past
the ordinary habits of youth.

There is no Old Spice now
to hide and mingle with nature,
and nature is leaving its heavy mark.
A tomcat spraying every corner.

Where I lay to sleep – the old man has been.
The sofa, the kitchen chair
the truck I borrow to get away for a moment
to buy wine
and further fortify my distance at night.

I whispered to her, "he needs a bath."
And she discretely told him,
then he announced his intention to me
thus completing the circle of this small conspiracy.

He is returning to nature now.
There is less distance between him
and the mildewed trees,
the dark dirt, the wildness
that creeps on the ground toward the farm house
as his mower takes less lawn each year.

Proof that we are not holy by being
but only in devotion. We are feral.

List

All the things I need to do
are lined up on the paper.
The paper itself is lined.
I scratched into each line
one thing that needs to be done.
But I haven't started yet
because I'm lying here in bed alone,
the air conditioner is blowing cold air at me
and it's warm here in the bed.
The coffee has not coursed
its way through me yet.
So I'll stay here and write little bits
until the coffee tells the air conditioner
to go to hell
and that I have a life
and there are things that need doing.

Sleep Part 2

Sleep has become scarce.
It could be the alcohol.
It might be the years
behind me.

It's a fitful and incomplete endeavor.
I roll back and forth.
Dreams nag at me
until I wake.

The dreams are not deep.
They're more like thoughts
that I want to push away
but busy themselves at me.
They are cats that want
to sleep in my bed
pawing and mewing.

Naps help
to fill the pail back up.
But I do miss the glorious
deep pull of my younger self
when I worried more
fretted more
but found escape in
the bottomless dark hours.
Now there is no escape
from myself
and my crooked and rocky
interior roads.

The Day After Thanksgiving

The rain on the day
after Thanksgiving
keeps some of the shoppers away.

This is a small blessing.

I just need some wood filler
and a new putty knife.
I'm not here to interrupt.
I don't want any trouble here.

Rope

Here we are
sitting on our lawn tractors
kitchen chairs
comfortable sofas
fabric protected
car seats
complaining
doing nothing.

We are black dogs
barking and barking
from an ever shortening
rope as it winds
around itself
until there is no
length left.

Wound

I hacked
at the strange bramble
with a curved blade saw
but my anger
at its stubbornness
caused me to miss the stump.

The arc ended at my shin
where an exact replica
of the saw's sharp teeth
imprinted in dripping red.

A chip of bone
seems to have moved
from its home
and there is a strange divot now
where the bone
should be smooth.

All of this is nothing
compared to the wound
she left me with.

Yawn

The great gape of space
between who you think you should be
and the machinations you perform
to become a version
of who you wish to be
is filled with your yawns.

Try a push-up or two.
Maybe a squat-thrust.
Blow on the coals.
Grab a wasp with your bare hand as it flies by.
Press your nose against the horse's neck.
Pound the hammer until the rock is dust.

Then take that dust
and make a statue
of yourself
and stop yawning.

Psychologist

It does not help
that I am faster
than him.

He runs ahead
for a bit
and I let him.

But when he thinks
he has gained ground
he turns to find me
in front of him
waiting for him to catch up.

And so I need
to look in the yellow pages
once again.

Snakes In The Woodpile

She asked me could
I move the wood.
The snakes had
taken over.

And so I moved it
piece by piece
my eyes peeled
for the shifting shape
that starts the letter
of their name.

But I have no fear
of snakes.
I've been one
myself before.
I know the
'Why' of their hiding.

Misunderstood
we are
to such
judgmental eyes.

Smarter People

You don't recognize them.
They sneak up on you.
I don't mean the academics.
I'm not talking about the people
who know something you don't know.
You can get yourself a book
and memorize those things
then you will know that something too.
I'm talking about the people
who make you see yourself
in a different way
the people who make you say
"I wish I had some of that."

Clock

The clock she keeps on counting
The mirror never lies
The lines they keep retreating
From around your eyes

Time she will be telling
All your dirty tricks
When horns begin to bellow
And heels begin to click

Come sleep eternal prayer
Come suffering no more
Come let's retire the player
Come tally up the score

Show all your limbs naked
Give up the final ghost
Tears will come no more
Your party's final toast

The sacred turned profane
The body just a shell
A suit to take a ride in
Another ne'er do well

An accidental meeting
From some ancient grip
We're all just here to feed
Until the scales finally tip

Fleeing

I sanded the walls
until my fingers bled.
I swore in silent
I would not do this job.
Then I continued for eighteen years
to cast myself into the thing I feared most –
a shadow.

A monochrome thing
swinging a hammer, turning a screw
cutting a sheet, lifting it high
holding it with my head
bleeding for another man's wealth.

But all the time I was assembling
bridges of song.
Some fell, some stood.
When enough
were built that I could cross
I dropped my tool belt
cursed the old man
and walked across the
labyrinth to a field
of soft grass.

There were thorns there
that I didn't expect.
But not enough to regret
my fleeing.

Bad Conversation

The problem
with all the words is that
so much of their
capacity depends
on the person
who is catching them
on the other end of the trapeze.

The Green Bike

I can smell it still.
It was cheaply made.
Some assembly was required.
Lime green but a deeper shade.

Fat tires,
white walls
ill-fitted white grips that moved
if I twisted my skinny wrists.

I was fearful.
My father's gentle taunting
did nothing to persuade
my steely mind.

I took the bike out in secret
and pushed along with my Keds
then somehow I was gliding.
I put my feet on the pedals.

I floated tentatively.
We were two skinny frames.
Then I pushed the pedals
and we became one machine.

All the gravel picked from my hands
the iodine stained knees
red-faced shame
disappeared and I rode.

Waiting For The Coffee

I'm lying here
prone
waiting for the coffee.

I like it very strong.
Hot.
I put a thimble of cream in.

Then I read a book
visiting
the palaces writers build.

It is the very best
part
of my day.

I'm in love with this
hour.
She has my heart fully.

Mowing

On the day John died
I mowed the yard.
Granite faced
to keep from crying.

He was a good man
as good a friend
as you can find
on our spinning rock.

Time and distance
had conspired that
we were friends
from many miles away.

But that long cable
to the past held strong.
I knew he was happy for me,
never voiced a jealousy…

That I had found my way
to the thing
we both loved so much as kids –
just to stand with a guitar.

And now every time I mow
I cannot *not* think of him.
He would find this funny
that he is my lawn-mowing ghost.

He would have a great one-liner
that would make me spit my beer
and that of course
would really get the laughing to boil.

And sometimes it's very hot
in Nashville where I mow the grass
and I pretend that it is sweat
running down my cheek
and not what it really is.

Worn

I'm worn.
The days drip by
while I try to keep up
on the conveyor belt.
The machinery
is well oiled.

My hands are soiled
from falling down
into the dirt
of a false rhyme
from that last line.
And that one too.

I've slowed
and will soon be towed
to the lousy writers' home
where the beer is warm
the keys on the typewriter stick
and operations are performed
with limb saws.

Conclusion

When the crow turns his oil black head
to look you in the eye

And the ivy
starts its arthritic crawl up your pant leg

When your fingers
are curled to a permanent frozen hook

You will know the ending
of the story, but not until then

It may come in gasping breath
or clutching heart, maybe a palsied shiver

It may arrive while you sleep
but we all will have our denouement

As sure as we look back
to see our footprints in the mud of our journey

A cliff awaits with loose ground
for our unsteady footing to discover

AUTHOR BIO

Rod Picott is a former construction worker turned award-winning singer-songwriter who has released ten albums since 2000. He has written a poetry collection *God in His Slippers* and a book of short stories *Out Past the Wires* both published by Mezcalita Press. Bestselling author Nicholson Baker said of *God in His Slippers*, "Life-loving poems that tell you what you need to know." Rod was born in New Hampshire, raised in Maine and has lived in Nashville for twenty-four years. He types with two fingers as he failed typing class – though excelled in English and Literature.

For more information on Rod Picott's work visit: www.rodpicott.com

MEZCALITA PRESS

An independent publishing company
dedicated to bringing the printed poetry,
fiction, and non-fiction of musicians who
want to add to the power and reach
of their important voices.

Visit us at: www.mezpress.com

www.ingramcontent.com/pod-product-compliance
Lightning Source LLC
Chambersburg PA
CBHW020944090426
42736CB00010B/1262